The Sutton Hoo Helmet

Sonja Marzinzik

THE BRITISH MUSEUM PRESS

First published in 2007 by
The British Museum Press
A division of The British Museum
Company Ltd
38 Russell Square
London WC1B 3QQ

www.britishmuseum.co.uk

A catalogue record for this book is available from the British Library

ISBN-13: 978-0-7141-2325-7
ISBN-10: 0-7141-2325-7

Designed by Esterson Associates
Typeset in Miller and
Akzidenz-Grotesque
Printed and bound in China
by C&C Offset

Acknowledgements
Warm thanks go to all the colleagues and friends who provided information, inspiration, comments, advice, images, accommodation and lovely meals: Alexandra & Frederik Sanmark, Angus Wainwright, Axelle Russo, Barry Ager, Christina Risberg, Coralie Hepburn, Gareth Williams, Jay Prynne, John Ljungkvist, Ian Meadows, Kate Sussams, Kevin Lovelock, Laura Lappin, Leslie Webster, Richard Hobbs, staff at the Gustavianum Museum, Uppsala, and Sylvia Sandelin, Stephen Crummy and Yun-chung & Gert Westermann-Li.

Extracts from *Beowulf: A Verse Translation* by Seamus Heaney reproduced with the kind permission of Faber and Faber Ltd.

Contents

NORTH SEA

York ●

Benty Grange ●

Snape
Wollaston ●   ●
Sutton Hoo ●

NORWAY

Vendel
Valsgärde
Gamla Uppsala

SWEDEN

Gotland

Torslunda
Öland

DENMARK

Deurne

300 kilometres
200 miles

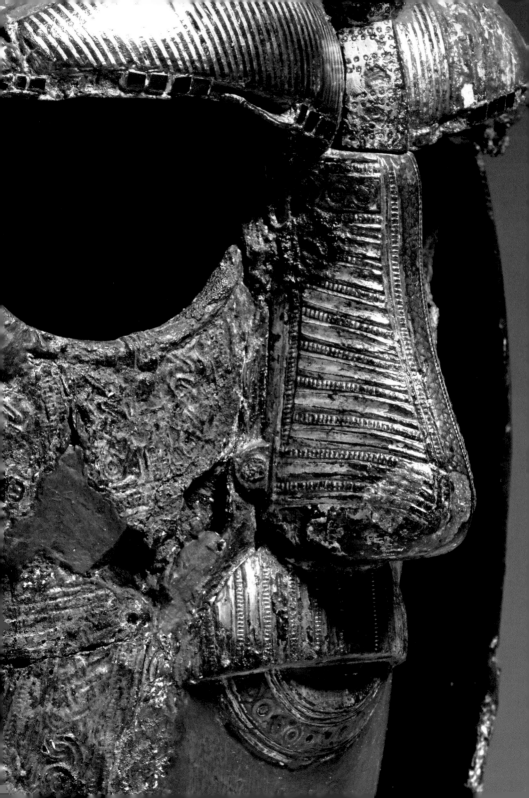

Prologue

A warrior's face, the strong brows inlaid with red garnets,
nose and mouth gilded and its surface tinned a silvery
colour – this is how the helmet found in the great mound
at Sutton Hoo once appeared to those who saw it (fig. 1).
It is more than just a fully functional helmet capable of
protecting its wearer in battle. The face mask would have
inspired awe and the intricate designs embossed on the
helmet plates might not have been mere decoration, but
may have lent another layer of protection to the wearer.
Today, some 1400 years after it was buried, its visual power
is still strong, making it one of the icons of the British
Museum. This book will tell the story of the discovery,
reconstruction and afterlife of this extraordinary object.

Chapter 1
A treasure is found

2 A view of the
excavated ship. The
ships rivets are visible
as clumps; compact
sand ghosts remained
of the planks and ribs.

Mrs Pretty gets curious

Edith Pretty was an energetic and inquisitive woman. During her youth she had travelled widely with her father and visits to Egypt had awakened her interest in archaeology and the past. After marrying in 1926, she and her husband moved to the Sutton Hoo estate in Suffolk (see map). They lived at Sutton Hoo House, a building situated dramatically on a plateau overlooking the River Deben.

After being widowed, Mrs Pretty decided to stay at Sutton Hoo and, in time, she returned to the interest of her youth: archaeology. Within eyesight of the house, a number of grave barrows were located (fig. 3). Recorded as early as 1601, there had been repeated episodes of probing, digging and burrowing into these mounds, but no proper archaeological investigation had ever taken place.

Her curiosity piqued, Mrs Pretty approached Guy Maynard, the curator of Ipswich Museum, on how to go about examining the mounds, which she believed had never been explored before. He recommended a local archaeologist called Basil Brown, who at the time was working for Ipswich Museum and who had extensive excavation experience in Suffolk. And so, in June 1938, Basil Brown started with a survey of the gravefield and its then known thirteen barrows.

The excavations begin

Brown settled on a medium-sized barrow, later known as Mound 3, as the first to be opened. Inside he found the cremated remains of a man and a horse and only a few disturbed remnants of numerous grave goods. These included fragments of an axe and the lid from a ewer that had come from the eastern Mediterranean.

The next mound, number 2, contained the first surprise. Despite having been heavily disturbed and robbed, it was possible to determine that a boat had been deposited in the barrow. Beneath it, a man was buried in a chamber with rich grave provisions. Again, only fragments remained, hinting at the original splendour. Among the finds were the tip of a pattern-welded sword, pieces from a blue glass vessel, silver-gilt drinking horn mounts and a silver buckle. Little, apart from some fine textile scraps and a bronze bowl that contained a cremation, was left in Mound 4.

With these discoveries, the 1938 field season came to a close. Although all three mounds had been robbed long before, what little was left showed that the graves had originally been well furnished. The style and types of objects pointed to the mid-sixth to seventh centuries AD and some of the objects had come from far away. The boat in Mound 2 provided a link to the burial and ship that had been discovered at Snape, one river-valley north of Sutton Hoo, in 1862. Mrs Pretty was obviously pleased, as she commissioned Brown to come back the following summer and continue the excavations.

A ship in the great mound

In May 1939 Brown was back on site at Mrs Pretty's request. Using the methodology he had developed the previous year, Brown, together with the gardener and the gamekeeper, began to make inroads into the largest mound, today known as the famous Mound 1. Brown followed an east-west axis, the same alignment as that of the burials in Mounds 2 and 3. Bearing in mind the remnants of a boat that had been found in Mound 2, he paid close attention to any changes in the colouring of the soil or the presence of ships rivets. When the first came to light on 11 May, Brown knew that he was on the right track. He plotted all further progress carefully and his diary reflects his excitement:

Have been working lately from 5.00 a.m. (when soils can be best studied) until late at night. Mr. Guy Maynard came over and agreed that such a find is unique in this country. Ship-burials have, of course, been found but not so good as this.

3 A view of the burial
mounds at Sutton Hoo.

Mrs Pretty, Brown noted, was 'greatly interested', but hopes for an untouched burial seemed slim. All previous graves on the site had been looted, the western flank of Mound 1 showed some disturbance and at the end of May Brown found traces of a pit that had been dug from the crown of the barrow. Pottery sherds inside the hole suggested that this happened in the late sixteenth or early seventeenth centuries. But the robbers had given up, never getting near the burial deposit.

By June, word had got around 'the archaeological establishment' of an important discovery at Sutton Hoo. Guy Maynard of Ipswich Museum visited regularly and on 6 June Charles Phillips, a fellow of Selwyn College, Cambridge, came to the site.

Brown, who reached the first object in the collapsed burial chamber amidships on 14 June, decided not to excavate it, but continued to clear the remainder of what would turn out to be a 27-metre vessel (fig. 2). He had had the foresight to leave each ship rivet in its place. These and

the compacted impressions the wood had left behind in
the sand indicated the planking of the ship, which was
about 4.5 metres wide.

The following month the Ancient Monuments
Inspectorate of the then Office of Works asked Charles
Phillips to take over the site. Admirably, Basil Brown tried
to see the positive side of this change and noted in his diary
on the day that Phillips and his team arrived, Monday 10
July:

Phillips will apparently act as representative of the Office
of Works here .... . Anyway I shall not have so much bother
and responsibility now in case anything went wrong.
I think I shall be able to co-operate all right, at least
I hope so.

Excavation of the burial chamber began and 263 objects
were lifted and documented. Meanwhile, the political
situation in Europe was deteriorating and the works
at Sutton Hoo continued under time pressure.

The burial chamber
Little remained of the timbers that had formed a
substantial chamber across the middle of the ship. It was
about 4.5 metres wide and 5.5 metres long and had been
covered by a roof. Inside the rectangular space, unexpected
and amazing wealth awaited discovery.

After a number of seemingly unclassifiable iron and
wooden objects, the first notable find was a large silver dish
on 20 July. Following this, weapons and a shield (fig. 26),
a heavy gold belt buckle (fig. 25), a pair of intricate shoulder
clasps (fig. 4), a chain-mail shirt, further Byzantine silver
dishes, gold coins, a cauldron and drinking vessels were
only some of the most important goods they recovered.
Colourful textiles in the form of clothes, furnishings, floor
and wall coverings, of which only few traces survived,
rounded off the ensemble. What was lacking completely,
however, were traces of a body (see Chapter 4). The
excavators proceeded cautiously, their efforts blighted
by poor weather and heavy rainstorms.

The discovery of the helmet

On 28 July the team came upon a scattering of iron
fragments, found not far from the shield boss and mounts
and just north of the beautiful shoulder clasps. Its position
on the original plan is indicated as an approximately round
area. Had there been a body, we would assume that the
scatter was positioned next to the head. It was immediately
clear what the scatter represented, as Charles Phillips wrote
in his excavation diary:

> The crushed remains of an iron helmet were found ... .
> The remains consisted of many fragments of iron covered
> with embossed ornament of an interlace type with which
> were also associated gold leaf, textiles, an
> anthropomorphic face-piece consisting of a nose, mouth,

and moustache cast as a whole (bronze) and bronze zoomorphic mountings and enrichments.

A few more fragments were found during the following day. All was boxed up and sent to the British Museum with a large consignment of other finds at the end of July, where they were to be cleaned and conserved.

The Treasure Trove inquest

While the excavation still continued, preparations for the Treasure Trove inquest were underway. Any gold and silver finds hidden in the ground with the intent to recover them belonged to the Crown, according to the law current in 1939. Two policemen visited the site on 11 August to inspect the excavation and three days later the public Coroner's court took place in the village hall at Sutton. Many of the gold and silver finds were exhibited in a glass case and fourteen jurors were to decide whether the objects from the Sutton Hoo ship burial had been buried covertly, with the intent of recovery, or not. They agreed on the latter and consequently the finds belonged to the landowner.

For a short time it looked as though the Crown might challenge this decision. Charles Phillips noted in his diary for 19 August:

> In the early evening I had an important conversation with Mrs. Pretty in which she announced her intention of presenting all the finds to the nation and authorised me to get the British Museum officials to publish this fact without delay.

And so the matter was settled. The excavation concluded on 25 August after the remains of the ship had been protected with a thick layer of bracken, but the trench was not backfilled. Within a fortnight the impending war broke out. So, not long after the finds had arrived in the British Museum, they left again, securely packed in crates for safekeeping in a disused tube tunnel at Aldwych in London.

In October 1939 an internal report to the British Museum's Trustees described Mrs Pretty's donation as 'the most magnificent and munificent single gift ever' made to the Department of British & Mediaeval Antiquities. In November the Keeper of that department, Thomas Kendrick, submitted another report concerning Sutton Hoo. He had been very aware of the immense pressure on Edith Pretty to keep the finds in Suffolk and that her decision had put her in a difficult position. Kendrick asked the Trustees 'if they would consider recommending in the proper quarter that some honour be conferred on Mrs. Pretty by the King'. But Mrs Pretty declined any such offer and the suggestion was not taken forward.

Chapter 2
The reconstruction of the helmet

Once peace had been declared, the crates returned to the British Museum. It took several years to unpack and reconstruct all the major objects, among them the helmet. Research on the objects found in Mound 1, its immediate and wider landscape context, as well as conservation and reconstruction were carried out under the auspices of Rupert Bruce-Mitford, then an assistant keeper in the Department of British & Mediaeval Antiquities at the British Museum. Even today his three-volume publication is the authoritative source on the ship burial.

A gigantic jigsaw puzzle

The helmet had been found shattered into a myriad of iron pieces, with only the cast bronze eyebrows, nose, mouth and moustache of the face mask immediately recognizable. Although in fragments, it seemed that not much distortion had occurred. This suggested that the burial chamber had held up for a substantial amount of time, allowing the helmet to oxidize, or rust, completely. Thus, when the chamber finally collapsed, the helmet just broke into many small pieces, rather than becoming squashed and deformed as it would have been if the chamber had collapsed shortly after the burial took place. So while it was an enormous task to reassemble this gigantic jigsaw puzzle, the fragmentation had in one way actually made it easier.

A first reconstruction of the helmet was modelled onto a plaster head. Like several of the other reconstructed objects, it was finished by 1947 and went on display (fig. 5). This manifestation of the helmet was somewhat awkward. For instance, the face mask had overly large eye openings and was fixed at an odd angle. Moreover, the small ear-flaps and rigid neck guard would have awarded little protection to the wearer.

17

6 *Previous pages*
Some of the helmet fragments after the first reconstruction was dismantled, which took four months.

7 *Below* Detail of the two opposing dragon heads at the front of the helmet in side view.

8 *Opposite* Front view of the helmet. The fluted strips are visible on the original fragments and are indicated by lines on the modern base.

The re-reconstruction

After much further research, which took better account of similar late Roman and Scandinavian helmets (see Chapter 3), Bruce-Mitford decided that it was time to dismantle the first reconstruction and start anew. The helmet fragments inset into the plaster backing were removed with the utmost care. Over 500 fragments, not all of which had been incorporated during the first restoration, were laid out (fig. 6).

Many of them were at first glance hardly more than nondescript pieces of iron. On some, the remains of decorated bronze sheets were preserved. These so-called repoussé sheets had been embossed with designs using die stamps. While some of the panels carried animal interlace patterns, others showed bits of figural scenes. Each decorative panel was held to the iron skull cap of the helmet and separated from the next embossed sheet by a grid of fluted bronze strips that were riveted in place (fig. 8).

Nigel Williams, the conservator who undertook the herculean task of piecing the helmet back together, spent two months scrutinizing the pieces, noting any decoration and differences in curvature. He could distinguish three different thicknesses among the fragments. Later on these would turn out to represent the skull cap, face mask and cheek pieces. Bits that had come from the edge were recognizable by a U-shaped binding or the marks it had left where it was missing.

Work progressed slowly, but a breakthrough came when the crest running across the top of the helmet was restored to its correct form. This dictated the dimensions of the helmet. The crest itself is a hollow iron tube inlaid with silver wires, which form a geometric pattern across its length, changing to scales at either end. The crest terminates in a dragon head both at the front and back (fig. 7).

Williams re-examined all X-rays, looking for matching joins. He noted that no lines were visible that would have indicated that the helmet had originally been constructed from sections.

Then, step by step, the various embossed sheets were identified. There were two different interlace designs, one

9 Drawing of the narrow interlace motif.

on long narrow panels (fig. 9), the other on larger rectangular ones. Of the three figural scenes that emerged, only two could be reconstructed. The first one shows two warriors apparently dancing, crossing their sword arms and holding spears (fig. 10). The other figural bronze sheet depicts a battle, in which a warrior on horseback, who is brandishing a spear, is driving his mount over an enemy (fig. 11). He, however, has raised his sword and is plunging it into the breast of the horse. Perched on the horse's rump, a small figure is holding onto the rider's spear, perhaps helping him to thrust it.

Gradually it was possible to reunite matching fragments. Minute traces of gold were detected on parts of the two fluted strips fitting along either side of the crest. This helped to determine the position of further fragments, as none of the remaining strips were gilded.

Other members of the Sutton Hoo research team were on occasion invited to look at some of the trickier joins with fresh eyes. Good progress was made and large parts of the right ear-flap and skull cap, then of the left side could be placed. It turned out that the design was identical on both halves of the skull cap. This, together with the varying thickness, curvature and patterning that Williams had noted, could now be used to put more fragments into place.

The reconstruction of the face mask proved to be simpler as the rough positions of the gilt bronze eyebrows and nose, which was cast in one with the mouth and moustache, were clear. On completion of the face mask, it became apparent that there was a rather unsatisfactory gap left between the brows, but the problem could not be resolved for the moment.

Only a few bits of the left ear-flap had survived and the last part to receive attention was the neck guard. The number of fragments which belonged here had been narrowed down to seventeen, characterized by their common thickness.

Rebuilding the helmet

More than nine months had passed and it was now possible to locate the assembled fragments onto a special plaster

10 The dancing warrior panel. Dotted lines are reconstructed.

11 The mounted warrior panel. The shaded areas are original.

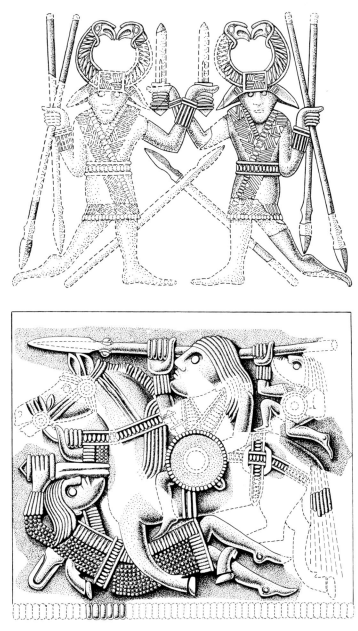

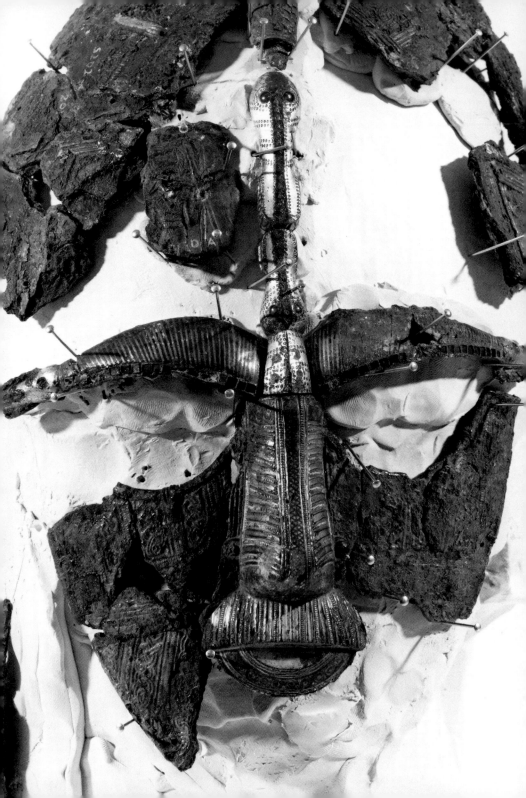

dome covered with oil-free plasticine (fig. 12). Initially most fragments had been joined with a soft adhesive. Over the next few weeks these reassembled complexes and further loose fragments were positioned on the dome with the help of long pins stuck into the plasticine.

The missing areas between the fragments were filled with adhesive-stiffened textile that was glued to the edges of the iron fragments. The textile was then covered with a very thin layer of plaster of Paris to achieve a smooth surface that was level with the iron fragments. The result was a finished cap that could be taken off the plasticine. As the backs of the original pieces remained unaffected, they could still be examined. The edges of the original elements were carefully protected with resin before the plaster of Paris was applied and they could easily be removed from their textile

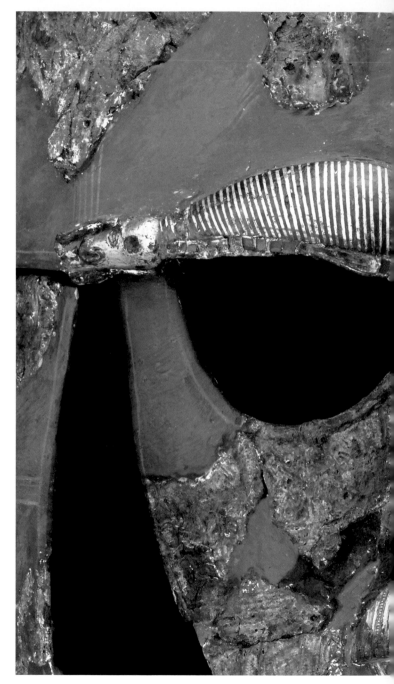

14 The flying dragon formed by the features of the face.

surrounds by using an appropriate solvent. This ensures that the pieces could be examined or receive conservation treatment if necessary and that the modern materials could be replaced should they start to deteriorate.

The cheek pieces were now added, at first with the cut-away edges nearest the face, as they had been on the first reconstruction. An arms and armour expert thought that they should be swapped over. Thus, they fitted perfectly with the curve of the neck guard, giving the wearer freedom to move his arms (fig. 13). Once the ear-flaps had been tied under chin, the head would have been fully protected.

It was time to fix the face mask to the helmet. It was discovered that one of the dragon heads fitted neatly into the gap between the eyebrows (see fig. 7). The features of the face now formed the striking image of a bird-like creature in flight: the garnet-set eyebrows were its wings, the nose its body and the moustache its tail (fig. 14). That left one of the other dragon heads for the front of the crest and the remains of the third one for its rear end.

The last step to completion was to paint all the infills brown to match the corroded appearance of the iron fragments. Lines were added to the modern parts in order to indicate missing panels. After eighteen months of hard work the helmet had been resurrected to a semblance of its original form. Its return to display on 2 November 1971 was announced with a press release and this reconstruction is still shown in the galleries.

The helmet as it looks today

Across the crown of the helmet runs the crest with the two dragon heads at either end. The crest was made from iron that was possibly blackened to provide a striking contrast with the silver inlay patterns. The dragon heads at either end were made from gilt bronze, with cabochon garnets for eyes, although the dragon at the back is now largely reconstructed. This dragon head seems to have been damaged and repaired in antiquity, suggesting that the helmet had been in use for some time before it was buried. However, claims that it was some 100 years old when it was laid down in the ship are unfounded in the light of recent chronological studies of comparable finds from Scandinavia and a recent reassessment of the coins from Sutton Hoo (see below).

The crest was not only a decorative feature, but would have helped to deflect blows to the head. This function is ascribed to the *wala* in *Beowulf* (lines 1029–33), an Anglo-Saxon poem composed some time between the seventh and tenth centuries AD:

> An embossed ridge, a band lapped with wire [wala] arched over the helmet: head-protection to keep the keen-ground cutting edge from damaging it when danger threatened and the man was battling behind his shield.

Until the Sutton Hoo discovery scholars had wondered about the exact meaning and translation of *wala*. The reconstruction process had now made this clear.

The helmet would have had a silvery skull cap, accentuated with gold, as the decorative and plain panels covering its surface were originally tinned and some of the fluting, the outer edging and the features of the face were gilded. Its appearance must have been striking and resembled very much another description given in *Beowulf* (lines 1447-54):

> To guard his head he had a glittering helmet …. It was of beaten gold, princely headgear hooped and hasped by a weapon-smith who had worked wonders in days gone by … and adorned it with boar-shapes; since then it had resisted every sword.

The central focus at the front was the flying bird motif formed by the facial features. The eyebrow-wings have boar's-head terminals and were made from gilded bronze inlaid with silver wires and edged with garnets. On close examination in the British Museum it became clear that they are not identical. While the garnets on the right eyebrow are backed with stamped gold foils that would have reflected light and given the stones a certain glow,

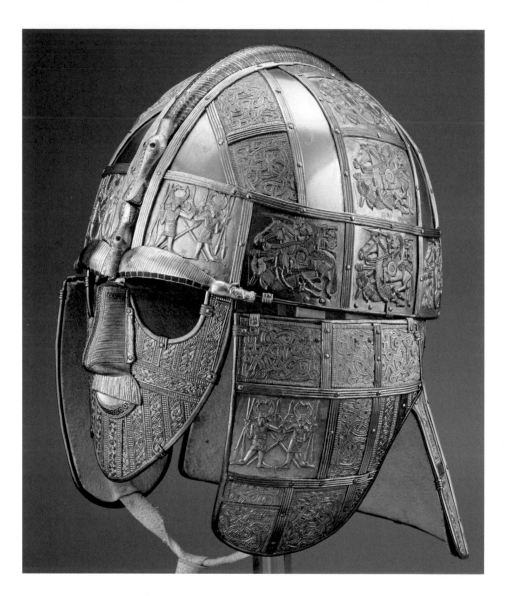

15 The replica, showing the order of the different repoussé panels.

there are no foils on the left brow, which is also slightly shorter than the other one. In addition, the gilding on both brows seems to be slightly different. The reason for these discrepancies is unknown. Perhaps the left brow was repaired at some point, but this is by no means certain. The nose and mouth piece were gilded and details of the ornament were picked out in silver wire inlay. Although the hollow nose is not large enough to fit over a real nose, the two holes drilled into its underside would have helped with breathing behind the mask.

The remainder of the mask was covered by the narrow interlace panels. Likewise, the neck guard was only decorated with interlace, although both patterns are found here. The cheek pieces contained in addition one of the figural scenes, the dancing warriors. Around the lower edge of the skull cap the mounted warrior panels are arranged, while directly above the eyebrows the dancing warriors are shown again. finally, plain fields alternate with stripes of interlace panels and the rider motif towards the crest of the helmet.

While the face mask was rigid, the cheek pieces and neck guard were attached to the helmet cap by leather hinges. These were fixed to the metal by small rivets, which are still visible in some places. It is clear that the helmet would have had a lining, not only to offer more comfort, but also to provide some cushioning in case of a blow to the head. The inside of the iron helmet fragments was corroded in an unusual way, differing from other iron objects retrieved from the burial. This is probably due to the remains of a leather lining inside the helmet cap.

The replica

In the 1971 press release on the new reconstruction the plan to create a replica of the helmet was announced. It was to be produced by the Royal Armouries, which were then based at the Tower of London. The goal was not only to give a true impression of what the helmet would have looked like, but also to assess its practical aspects and to investigate the crafts process (fig. 15).

From a technological point of view, the replica differs from the original in a small number of details, which facilitated the manufacture. Its appearance, however, is a faithful rendition of the helmet's original appearance. At 3.74 kg, including the chamois leather lining, the replica is somewhat heavier than the original would have been. A weight of around 2.5 kg has been estimated for the latter.

Chapter 3

The family tree of the Sutton Hoo helmet

16 The helmet from
Valsgärde, Sweden,
grave 7 (height *c.* 33 cm).

When the first provisional guide to the Sutton Hoo ship burial was published in 1947, a section was dedicated to the helmet. Already it was noted that it was 'similar to those found in Swedish boat-graves at Vendel and Valsgärde'. At these two sites in the Uppland province north of Stockholm numerous graves containing ships, weapons and helmets or remains thereof had been excavated from 1881 onwards. They cover a long time span, with the earliest burials dating to the first half of the sixth century and the latest ones to about the first half of the eighth century. The importance of the burials was such that the early medieval period in Sweden from AD 550 to AD 800 is now called the Vendel Period.

Scandinavian crested helmets

Due to both their distribution in Scandinavia and the decorative ridge running over the top, these helmets are now known as the Nordic crested group. The Sutton Hoo helmet fits in well with this type. More or less complete examples or characteristic fragments have been found in Uppland and other parts of Sweden, including the isle of Gotland, with a small number originating from Britain, Norway, Denmark and outside Scandinavia. Their date span covers the eighth to tenth centuries. All are highly individual pieces of varying constructive principles, ornate and at the same time practical. Unifying features of the group are the presence of the crest with its animal-head terminals, the prominent eyebrows and on numerous helmets also the fluted strips separating the decorative embossed sheets with often strikingly similar motifs.

The Sutton Hoo helmet is distinguished by a crest which is wire-inlaid and iron rather than engraved bronze, as is more common in Scandinavia. It is unique in having been raised from a single sheet of iron. The assumption that it was made like this is based on the complete absence of any

17 A warrior wearing a helmet as shown on one of the Torslunda die stamps.

joins that would suggest that it was built up from separate elements held by broad bands, as all the other helmets are. Also unparalleled are the large mask covering the entire face and the leather-hinged cheek pieces and broad neck guard.

It should, however, not be forgotten that the decorative panels on some of the helmets from Vendel and Valsgärde and two of the die stamps for the production of embossed sheets from Torslunda on the Swedish isle of Öland show warriors wearing exactly such helmets (fig. 16).

Beowulf again demonstrates that face masks seem to have been well-known helmet components (lines 255–7):

The hard helmet, hasped with gold, will be stripped of its hoops; and the helmet-shiner who should polish the metal of the war mask sleeps ... .

As for similarities, the mounted warrior shown on the Sutton Hoo helmet is found in variations on the helmets from Valsgärde, graves 7 and 8. The dragon heads on the crest from grave 7 are strikingly close to those from Sutton Hoo and additionally the former helmet contains panels with the dancing warriors design, which has also been found at nearby Gamla Uppsala. The helmet from Vendel grave 14 has the same curved eyebrows with boar's-head terminals, although they are made from bronze. Here, too, a bird forms the bronze face mask, albeit sweeping downwards rather than upwards as on the English helmet, and less sophisticated in its execution. Moreover, several die stamps with related scenes were found at Torslunda. The variation between the nearly identical scenes and analogous but not identical constructions suggests that several independent workshops produced the helmets and their decoration. finally, numerous helmet fragments have been found on Gotland. These include two sets of iron eyebrows with wire inlay just like on those from Sutton Hoo. They are from Hellvi and Halla parishes in northern and central Gotland and the latter also yielded parts of an iron cheek piece and a probable face mask.

Much has been made of how unusual the surface finish of the Sutton Hoo helmet supposedly was. The tinning, however, is also found on the Valsgärde grave 6 helmet, where traces of a whitemetal coating are still visible. As recent enquiries have shown, it appears that none of the Scandinavian helmets underwent the complex scientific investigation which detected the Sutton Hoo tinning, so more surprises may yet be in store.

The exact nature of the connection between the Sutton Hoo helmet and its Scandinavian 'cousins' is unclear. Was the helmet made by Scandinavian craftsmen working in East Anglia? Or, less likely, were just the dies used to stamp the designs onto the bronze sheets from Scandinavia? We should not exclude the possibility that the whole helmet might have been made there. The strong similarities in the execution of details as well as the congruence of the repoussé motifs certainly indicate that whoever made the helmet knew more than one piece from this group.

The connection between Sutton Hoo and Scandinavia, in particular Sweden, extends beyond the helmet. A number of features occur in both areas. Boat graves and the burial or at least cremation of a large assemblage fit for a man of some standing, for instance. Other, more specific, commonalities are the type of boss and decorative elements of the shield, the scene of a man between beasts on the lid of the purse (fig. 18) and the deposition of intricate chains for suspending cauldrons suitable for cooking feasts in. The sheer wealth of the undisturbed burial of Sutton Hoo Mound 1 is, however, unsurpassed.

Antecedents of the Sutton Hoo helmet

But the family tree of the Sutton Hoo helmet reaches further than just to Scandinavia. The Swedish professor Sune Lindqvist studied the helmets from Vendel in great detail. In 1925 he was the first to draw attention to the parallels between Nordic crested helmets and late Roman helmets. He noticed the similarity in construction between the Vendel pieces and a late Classical helmet from the Netherlands, which came to light in a peat bog known as 'The Peel' near the village of Deurne (fig. 19).

The peat cutter who found it put it on show in his living room and eventually sold it to the National Antiquities

19 The silver-gilt fourth-century AD helmet from Deurne, Netherlands (height 28.5 cm).

Museum in Leiden. Lundqvist came to the conclusion that such late Roman models were the antecedents of the early medieval examples. Bruce-Mitford's research confirmed this suggestion and added further pieces of evidence.

One possible link between late Roman helmets and their derivations in the Germanic world are military adventurers. The late Roman army comprised countless Germanic mercenaries, who could rise to high ranks. It seems that they took to their head gear, which may have accompanied them home after the end of their service. Other helmets may have been loot or gifts. Thus the various types were proliferated, modified and developed also in areas outside the Roman and later the Byzantine empires.

Other English helmets

Although helmets are rare among early medieval finds, the Sutton Hoo helmet is not the only example we know from Anglo-Saxon England.

In 1848 a once richly furnished but robbed burial in a mound at Benty Grange in Derbyshire produced an iron framework that had originally been covered with horn plates. A cross decorated the long nasal but the most striking feature was a small copper alloy boar with garnet eyes and gilded tusks that adorned the top of the crest. This figure is again reminiscent of *Beowulf* (lines 303–6):

> So they went on their way. ... Boar-shapes flashed above their cheek-guards, the brightly forged work of goldsmiths, watching over those stern-faced men.

Furthermore, on some of the Scandinavian helmet panels and on one of the dies from Torslunda, helmets crowned with boar figures are depicted. The find from Benty Grange illustrates that *Beowulf* and these images were not just artistic conventions but did reflect reality. A mid-seventh-century date for the Derbyshire grave makes it a near contemporary of Sutton Hoo.

Building works in Coppergate, York, led to a spectacular discovery in 1982. A copper and brass helmet in surprisingly good condition lay at the bottom of a wood-

lined pit. It is likely that the pit was a well. The manner in which the helmet was put down implies that someone had carefully deposited it, presumably with the intent to recover it, but did not manage to do so before the pit eventually infilled.

The Coppergate helmet preserves faithfully some of the characteristics of earlier crested helmets, such as the pronounced, grooved eyebrows and the crest ending in an animal head terminal at the front, even if it uses an entirely different style. In its construction it closely resembles the Scandinavian pieces. A nose-to-nape and two lateral bands were riveted to a broad brow band. The gaps in between were then filled with triangular plates, resulting in the helmet cap. Eyebrows and a nasal were added in one piece and like the Sutton Hoo helmet the Coppergate example had ear-flaps, albeit fixed with metal hinges. Chain-mail for protection of the neck is again a feature more akin to the Scandinavian finds, where mail curtains sometimes covered the neck and face below a visor. Unique to the York helmet is a Latin inscription running from nose to nape and repeated on a band perpendicular to the crest. The undoubtedly Christian text also names a man called Oshere, perhaps the owner or maker of the helmet.

The Coppergate helmet was made between *c.* AD 750 and 775 and is therefore one of the latest examples of a Nordic crested helmet to be found. However, depictions of crested helmets in manuscripts, on sculpture and on coins imply that the type was still popular up to the early eleventh century in England.

The most recent find came to light in 1997 (fig. 20). Quarrying activities at Wollaston, near Wellingborough in Northamptonshire, triggered the discovery of the so-called 'Pioneer' helmet, nick-named after the gravel extraction firm who funded its conservation treatment. Archaeologists were already on site investigating a Roman road and working closely with a metal detectorist who helped to survey the area. He picked up signals from what turned out to be the burial of a man who, it appears from the bones and teeth preserved, was less than twenty-five years old. He had been laid out carefully on some sort of bedding, a fine textile

20 The helmet from Wollaston, Northamptonshire, with its boar crest (height *c.* 36 cm).

and possibly a mattress and pillow. The grave, perhaps under a mound, was located by the side of the road, although it is not entirely clear whether it was still in use in the seventh century when the burial took place. A sword, several buckles, a small clothing hook and a slightly battered hanging bowl accompanied him. The most surprising find was an iron helmet with hinged cheek pieces. It had been set down by the man's left hip and rolled over at some point.

Interestingly, it had been 'ritually killed' before it was placed in the grave: the nasal was bent back into the helmet, using so much force that the metal had fractured.

Subsequent ploughing damaged the helmet severely and most of its right-hand side along with parts of the back are now missing. It seems that the helmet surface was plain apart from groups of incised lines. As opposed to the Sutton Hoo and other early medieval helmets, the Wollaston piece was therefore much more strongly focused on functionality than on display. But, like Benty Grange, it had a boar crest. In terms of its construction the Wollaston helmet is, however, closer to the York find.

We may expect that in time further helmets will be unearthed. For instance, a terminal in the shape of a boar's head from Horncastle in Lincolnshire might have come from a helmet crest and a small boar figure belonged to an old grave find from Guilden Morden, Cambridgeshire. Two further possible crest fragments were found at Icklingham in Suffolk and Rempstone in Nottinghamshire. And a silver foil fragment from Caenby, Lincolnshire, shows a man in a horned headdress resembling the dancing warriors from Sutton Hoo. But horned headdresses are also depicted on other objects, for example on a buckle plate from finglesham, Kent, and on a copper-alloy fragment from Ayton in Berwickshire, so we cannot be sure that the Caenby fragment really belonged to a helmet.

Helmets in the early Middle Ages

As the above discussion shows, helmets are not common in early medieval burials. We now know of more than 100,000 Germanic inhumation burials dating to about the fifth to seventh centuries AD. Spear heads and shield bosses and even the sword and the so-called seax or short-sword are not rare. But we only know of some thirty-seven crested helmets or parts thereof and of about fifty-five examples of other types. All in all, it seems that evidence survived for fewer than a hundred helmets from the fifth to eleventh centuries AD.

While the crested helmets are a Nordic phenomenon, the so-called *Spangenhelme*, *Lamellenhelme* and other types have also been found in France, Germany, Italy and the Balkans. There are even three examples from Kiev and north Africa.

Spangen helmets are named after four to six distinctive T-shaped mounts, or *Spangen*, that form the outer framework of the helmet. Almond-shaped plates are riveted to the inside of the framework, filling the gaps between the T-mounts. Although their roots may lie in Sasanian Persia, these helmets were produced in the armouries of the Byzantine Empire and also in Italian manufactories that continued production after the Ostrogothic conquest of AD 488/9. They were originally meant for the Byzantine army but would have found their way into the Germanic world via the mercenaries mentioned above, as gifts or loot. Where *Spangen* helmets occur in graves, these are usually richly furnished and date between the late fifth century and around AD 600.

Overlapping lamellae, which could be made from horn or sometimes metal, give their name to the *Lamellen* helmets of the sixth century. Often the only archaeologically visible remains are the metal knob from the peak of the helmet and the brow plate with the nasal. Lamella constructions for both helmets and body armour are a trait introduced by eastern nomadic peoples such as the Huns and the tradition is carried on beyond the early Middle Ages, up to the Mongols in the thirteenth century.

Both *Spangen* and lamellar helmets have hinged cheek pieces and a mail curtain that protects the neck. The latter detail was taken up in some of the Scandinavian examples and ultimately also in the York helmet.

Helmets in early medieval literature and art

In the Roman army every legionary wore a helmet, as written sources, graffiti of owners' names on excavated helmets and the large number of finds show. The situation for the Byzantine army may have been similar. The *Codex Theodosianus* is a compilation of old imperial laws and was published in AD 438. In Book X, Chapter 22.1 it notes a decree issued in AD 374. It states that each craftsman in the armouries of Constantinople and Antioch had to

21 The right-hand panel of the Franks Casket shows an armed and helmeted warrior in a forest.

decorate six helmets and their cheek guards with gold and silver ornaments in a month. Although these were probably officers' helmets, the general output levels implied would have been sufficient to equip whole army units.

For all we know, this was significantly different in the Germanic areas during the early Middle Ages. The small number of known helmets in connection with the often well-equipped if not extraordinary grave contexts they come from suggest that they were some sort of status symbol not available to everyone. This does not necessarily mean that the Anglo-Saxons and other Germanic peoples shunned head protection in battle. For instance, sturdy leather caps, perhaps additionally strengthened with horn plates, could have been used and would only under exceptional circumstances have left traces in the archaeological record.

Images of helmets are as rare as the objects themselves, but they do exist. A mounted warrior, apparently wearing a *Spangen* helmet with a waving plume, is depicted on a late sixth-century silver plate from Isola Rizza near Verona. Another Italian find is a brow plate from a lamellar helmet from Val di Nievole near Lucca. The copper-gilt plate, with an inscription naming the Longobard king Agilulf, portrays him seated between two warriors of his guard. Both of these wear helmets, again with fluttering plumes. A small number of Ostrogoth coins are difficult to assess. They show kings with a headdress that could be a helmet or, perhaps more likely, an early form of crown.

Manuscripts and objects which post-date the seventh century on occasion show helmets. At Aberlemno, Angus, Scotland, a sculpted stone depicts Pictish warriors, some of whom wear helmets with a large nasal. These helmets are not so dissimilar from those on the eighth-century Franks Casket which was carved from whalebone in Northumbria (fig. 21).

Moreover, several late Anglo-Saxon stone reliefs from the tenth century bear carvings of men with various helmet forms, notably one from Sockburn, Durham, with a definitely crested type. From then onwards pointed forms become dominant and are illustrated on coins and in manuscripts. Depictions on Swedish runestones and artefacts suggest that there, too, pointed helmets came into fashion around the turn of the tenth to eleventh centuries.

Lastly, there is the Bayeux tapestry, which was made in the late eleventh century, perhaps the 1070s. It illustrates the pointed helmet with the addition of a nasal, a form typically associated with the Norman conquest. Although on the tapestry it is not exclusively restricted to the top echelons of those fighting, it appears that it is mainly the retinues of kings and nobles who are helmeted.

Early medieval authors mention helmets as well, albeit infrequently. The most detailed descriptions are found in *Beowulf*, as cited above.

Gregory of Tours, a bishop who wrote numerous works in the sixth century, reported that the Franks called the helmet *galea*, but it does not figure in his descriptions of common armament. The helmet also had a metaphorical meaning and Gregory compared the protection it affords directly to that which God would give. Moreover, he mentions that a nail from the cross of Christ adorned the helmet-crown of a statue of Constantine the Great, the first emperor to recognize Christianity officially. Otherwise, Gregory refers to helmets only twice, in connection with a nobleman and a military leader.

Isidore of Seville was another bishop and distinguished early medieval author. By the time of his death in AD 636 he had compiled a twenty-volume encyclopaedia covering all areas of life and learning of his era. One of the chapters, dedicated to 'War and Games', has a very brief section on helmets, in which he explains what the different parts of a *galea* are called. Interestingly, he mentions that a *crista* – a crest or plume – crowns the top of a helmet.

Added protection
It seems that the owners of helmets did not want to rely on their practical function alone. Additional protection was sought by emblazoning them with decoration that was more than purely ornamental.

Jupiter and Victory were sometimes depicted on the brow bands of Roman helmets. As the later *Spangen*

22 Drawing of a T-shaped *Spangen* mount with Christian decoration on a helmet from Stössen, Germany.

23 Detail from the Sutton Hoo helmet: the larger interlace panel at the top of the right cheek guard.

helmets were produced in Byzantine, i.e. Christian, workshops, their brow bands and T-shaped mounts are often covered with Christian symbols. Crosses are frequent, as are grapes and vine tendrils, which illustrate the Bible word of Christ as the vine (fig. 22).

Likewise, the York helmet's inscription is emphatically Christian and the Benty Grange helmet had a cross on the nasal. The boar figures on this helmet and the one from Wollaston might have symbolized notions such as strength and courage.

In the case of the Sutton Hoo helmet, five different motifs were used for the helmet panels, two interlace patterns (figs 9 and 23) and three figural scenes, only two of which we can decipher.

46

24 One of the dancing warriors above the Sutton Hoo helmet's proper right eyebrow.

Scholars still debate the meaning of interlace, but it has been suggested that beside its decorative qualities it might have been a way of binding evil by literally tangling it up in knots.

The mounted warrior scene, including all its Scandinavian and continental variants, is enigmatic. The small figure perched behind the rider holds on to his spear and seems to help him aim it. Despite this presumably divine helper, the rider does not notice that doom threatens in the form of an enemy plunging his sword from below into the breast of the horse. Some interpretations see this man as the fallen enemy who is overcome and making a desperate last thrust. But the oblivious nature of the rider has led to a suggestion that here we see a combat tactic described by the Roman writer Ammianus Marcellinus in the fourth century. His account of a battle involving the Germanic Alamans (Book XVI, Chapter 12.22) relates how their

> ... infantry soldier in the very hottest of the fight ... can creep about unseen, and by piercing a horse's side throw its unsuspecting rider headlong, whereupon he can be slain with little trouble.

So who is the victor, who the vanquished on the rider panels of the Sutton Hoo helmet?

The scene with the two warriors brandishing spears and sporting horned headdresses with bird's-head terminals seems easier to explain (figs 10 and 24). Such dancers have also been depicted elsewhere and they may be related to the cult of Woden, the Nordic god of war also known as Odin. In later written sources his companions are two ravens called Hugin and Munin and the spear is his symbol. Therefore, the Sutton Hoo scene could represent some sort of martial dance. It is possible that the motif of two dancing warriors goes back to late Roman models, just like the helmet form, as the divine twins Castor and Pollux in military uniform are occasionally found on the cheek pieces of late Classical helmets.

Chapter 4
The quest for the man buried in Mound 1

25 It is unknown where the great gold buckle from Sutton Hoo was made, but very similar forms were fashionable in Merovingian Gaul.

The impact of the discovery

When news of the extraordinary discovery at Sutton Hoo spread, it caused considerable excitement. The *East Anglian Daily Times* featured an article entitled 'Great archæological find in Suffolk: Details of the ship-burial near Woodbridge' on 29 July 1939. It enthused that

> A discovery which may go a long way to dispel the obscurity which at present enshrouds the early history of England, and therefore may be as important to this country as was the finding of the tomb of Tutankhamen to Egypt, has been made in Suffolk.

Not only the public but also scholars were amazed. The wealth of gold and silver in the burial was unparalleled in Britain. More importantly, the quality and beauty of the garnet jewellery and millefiori glass inlay in particular (see figs 4 and 18) and the complexity of the chain-mail and textiles demonstrated a sophistication unexpected from what was then called 'The Dark Ages'.

The international character of the assemblage made another crucial point: life in seventh-century eastern England was far from isolated and insular. The objects reflected connections to all of the then-known world. There

were silver bowls from the Byzantine empire, Frankish gold coins and a gold buckle with close parallels from Gaul (fig. 25), hanging bowls from the Celtic West and Scandinavian influences visible in the boat burial custom and in the helmet and shield (fig. 26).

The splendour of the Sutton Hoo burial illustrated that heroic poems such as *Beowulf* were not mere flights of fancy. Instead they reflected life, at least for the top tiers of society, more closely than it had ever been thought possible. Views of a primitive lifestyle in which the Germanic newcomers to Britain struggled to make ends meet had to be rethought almost overnight. Once it was reconstructed, the helmet played a particular role here. The complex construction and beautiful decoration surprised people with their intricacy. It literally put a face on the past, giving an immediacy to the early Middle Ages that is otherwise unsurpassed in the British Museum's collections of that period.

The lack of a body

Despite meticulous excavation, no body was found during the 1939 excavations. Speculations that the mound might have been a cenotaph – a commemorative monument rather than a burial – were soon discarded. In the acidic soils of East Anglia, at Sutton Hoo as well as elsewhere, often little more than small bone fragments or remains of the tooth crowns survive, so if there had been a body in Mound 1 it might well have disappeared completely.

During the re-excavation of the ship in 1965-7, soil samples were taken. As the phosphate levels were significantly higher inside the chamber than outside, it is reasonable that a body had lain in it once. The analyses could not, however, determine whether the source of the phosphate was human or animal, i.e. a sacrifice. The later campaigns at Sutton Hoo uncovered a number of 'sand people'. As bodies decomposed in the ground, their contours could be preserved as compact, darker shapes in the sand. They were difficult to see and too fragile to lift. But when the Mound 1 grave chamber had collapsed, perhaps as long as a hundred years after the burial, any remains of a body would

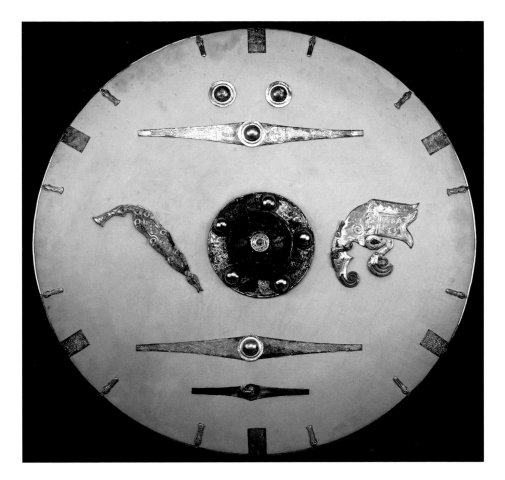

26 The Sutton Hoo shield. The closest parallels to the shield boss and fittings are found in Sweden.

have been shattered and it is unlikely that the bone debris would have left traces in the sand.

An alternative, although today not generally accepted, explanation for the lack of a body is that Mound 1 was for a cremation burial. On a large silver dish placed inside the burial chamber remains of ferric phosphate had been found. A likely source for this would have been charred or burnt bone, which could either have come from a joint of meat or represent a cremation deposit. Human cremations set down in bronze vessels have been found in other mounds at Sutton Hoo, so this possibility cannot be excluded, but it is equally impossible to prove it.

In any case, the large array of weapons and armour in the grave, a sword, several spears and lances, an axe-hammer, a shield, a mail coat and the helmet confirm that a man had found his last rest here.

'Who was he?'

The question now was who had been buried in the ship. It was certainly a great lord with all that would be appropriate for his standing: fine weapons, jewellery, treasure in the form of coins and silver plate, cooking and drinking vessels for banquets, a lyre for entertaining guests in the hall, gaming counters for leisurely passing the time and symbols of status such as the supposed whetstone-sceptre and standard. Thoughts quickly turned to one of the kings of East Anglia. Thomas Kendrick mentioned this idea in a letter to Edith Pretty on 2 August 1939:

> There is no doubt that the man in your barrow must have been a very important person and we're beginning to wonder if he was King Redwald of East Anglia!

The following year, the Cambridge historian Hector Munro Chadwick published an article under the title 'Who was He?' and he, too, argued for Raedwald as the most likely candidate.

Our main source on this potentate is the *Ecclesiastical History*, written by the monk Bede sometime before AD 731. Bede described Raedwald as an ambitious man, with plans beyond his own realm. He eventually became high-king (called *Bretwalda* in a ninth-century manuscript) of all Anglo-Saxon kingdoms in AD 616. It is not clear when he died, but generally it is assumed that this happened in AD 624 or 625. Raedwald was converted to Christianity on a visit to Kent but reverted to paganism when he returned home. According to Bede, he erected a Christian altar and next to it a smaller pagan one.

All this seemed to fit well with the ship burial, the apparently Christian hints in the pair of possible baptismal spoons and the sumptuous provisions that scholars considered clearly pagan. The main argument cited for

Raedwald were the thirty-seven Merovingian coins found in the burial. Twenty-four of these could be traced to specific minting places in Frankish Gaul. It was long thought that the likely date of the coins points to a deposition around AD 625, which would have fitted perfectly with the likely date of Raedwald's death. A recent reassessment of the coins suggests, however, that they cannot be dated so closely and that we can only say that a burial between *c.* AD 595 and *c.* AD 640 is likely.

This wider dating would open the door for a number of other contenders for Mound 1. For instance, one of Raedwald's successors mentioned in the written sources might be buried here. But it is entirely possible that a king not referred to in any historical account found his last resting place at Sutton Hoo. After all, coins with their names are the only evidence we now have for several East Anglian rulers of the eighth and ninth centuries.

To this day, we do not know for sure what an early medieval royal burial would have looked like. Therefore we must consider the possibility that this grave did not belong to a king at all. For example a West Saxon man called Mul was killed in AD 687. Although he was only the brother of a king, the *wergild* or compensation money that had to be paid for his murder was equal to that of an actual monarch. If we want to keep the association with known royalty, one candidate for Sutton Hoo would be Raegenhere, Raedwald's son, who was killed in battle in AD 616. We could imagine that Raedwald prepared this most splendid funeral for his son and heir.

And then there is of course the question of the robbed ship burial in Mound 2. Basil Brown had excavated it in 1938, it was re-examined in 1986-9 and it is thought that its original wealth was comparable to Mound 1.

Considering all these points, we cannot be sure who was buried with the helmet in Mound 1. There is no doubt that he was an outstanding man and whoever organized his funeral sought to express this status in the most dramatic way.

Epilogue

Further excavations

The 1939 discoveries were not the end of the story but the starting point for further research. The 1965-7 campaign under Rupert Bruce-Mitford concentrated mainly on the re-examination of the ship and a plaster cast with all the rivets *in situ* was produced. In the following four years various areas of the site were excavated. From 1983 to 1993 further comprehensive work and geophysical surveys took place under the auspices of Martin Carver. They were sponsored primarily by the Sutton Hoo Research Trust, which was specifically founded as the principal body to launch and advance the campaigns of the 1980s to 1990s.

It became clear that there were eighteen mounds as well as further graves, containing both cremation and inhumation burials. Some of these men and women had been laid to rest with what we consider high-status grave goods. Two groups of inhumation burials from about the eighth to the eleventh centuries attracted special attention. In both at least some individuals had lost their lives through hanging or beheading and others were buried with bound hands, suggesting that public executions took place at the mound cemetery. This is not particular to Sutton Hoo, as there are other places where prehistoric or early medieval barrows became the focus of late Saxon capital punishment.

Additional studies of the site and the surrounding landscape took into account prehistoric, Roman and medieval features and settlement patterns, environmental sequences and soil morphology. The aim was to gain a holistic picture of Sutton Hoo and to place it in a wider framework, considering not only its local and regional setting but also its wider Anglo-Saxon and European context.

In advance of building works at Sutton Hoo further investigation was necessary in the summer of 2000.

28 Swedish fish tins, books, stamps and journals are just some of the items using a likeness of the Sutton Hoo helmet.

THE
ANGLO-
SAXONS

EDITED BY JAMES CAMPBELL

LES BARBARES
ET LA MER

*CAEN
TOULOUSE*

Nineteen inhumations and seventeen cremations, some of them surrounded by ring ditches, were discovered. It appears that the cemetery started out in the first half of the sixth century. Among these graves, many were very well equipped, especially with weapons. Analysis of the site still continues, taking the history of research on Sutton Hoo into the twenty-first century.

Sutton Hoo today

Edith Pretty did not live to see the Sutton Hoo finds go on display. The *Woodbridge Reporter* announced the death of the 'national benefactress' in December 1942. The estate was sold three years later. The family, however, retained and still holds the right to excavate at Sutton Hoo.

Subsequently, Sutton Hoo was administered by the Annie Tranmer Charitable Trust. In 1998, this trust gave the 99-hectare estate with all its buildings, the grave field and a sizeable area of land to the National Trust. Today there is a visitor centre with a permanent exhibition on the ship burial (fig. 27). A full-size reconstruction of the grave chamber and replicas of objects from Mound 1 are on display. These fulfil Mrs Pretty's wish that copies should be made available so that the treasures she had donated to the nation could also be seen in Suffolk. In addition, archaeological objects from some of the other burials are on loan from the British Museum. The centre is situated at a short distance from the grave field and visitors can take a walk around the mounds, three of them now reconstructed to their original shape, and wander down towards the shore of the river Deben.

The Sutton Hoo helmet has lost none of its fascination. It adorns the cover of novels, scholarly and popular publications. Replicas, sometimes barely recognizable, can be bought over the internet and its discovery has inspired artists, film makers, designers and writers. J.R.R. Tolkien, for instance, had only written the first few chapters of the 'Lord of the Rings', when the 1939 excavations made headlines. He later repeatedly referred to the ship burial and it may well have influenced his description of barrow wights and the burial mounds of Rohan.

The Sutton Hoo helmet was featured in a special stamp series commemorating the 250th anniversary of the foundation of the British Museum (fig. 28). In 2006 its replica toured Asia, amazing audiences there. For many people, not just in Britain but far beyond, it has become the face of the early Middle Ages.

Glossary

Beowulf: An Anglo-Saxon epic
poem composed between the
seventh and tenth centuries
AD. It tells the story of the heroic
warrior Beowulf, his battles and
eventual death.

Cabochon: A gemstone or glass inlay
with a convex, smooth surface,
set singly.

Copper alloy: A mixture of copper
and other metals. Bronze is an
example of a copper alloy.

Fluted: Decorated with narrow,
parallel-running ribs.

Garnet: Red semi-precious stone.

The Merovingians: The Frankish
dynasty who ruled from the late
fifth century until AD 751.

Nasal: Narrow metal plate on
a helmet that protects the nose.

Niello: A black inlay usually made
from silver- or copper-sulphides.

The Picts: A people in north-eastern
Scotland mentioned in written
sources from the fourth to ninth
centuries AD.

Repoussé: Sheet metal impressed
(embossed) with a die from
the back.

Further reading

Rupert Bruce-Mitford's three volumes on the ship burial (1975–83) are still the main source on Mound 1. Next to them now stands Martin Carver's (2005) authoritative publication on Sutton Hoo and its context from *c.* 3000 BC up to AD 2001.

Almgren, B., 'Helmets, crowns and warriors' dress – from the Roman emperors to the chieftains of Uppland.' In Lamm, J.P. and Nordström, H.-Å. (eds), *Vendel Period Studies*. The Museum of National Antiquities, Stockholm, Studies 2 (Stockholm 1983), 11–16.

Arwidsson, G., *Die Gräberfunde von Valsgärde* I – III (Uppsala, Lund 1942–77).

Axboe, M., 'Copying in Antiquity: The Torslunda Plates.' In Häßler, H.-J. (ed.), *Studien zur Sachsenforschung* 6. Veröffentlichungen der urgeschichtlichen Sammlungen des Landesmuseums Hannover 34 (Hildesheim 1987), 13–21.

Brown, B., Excavation diary 1938–9. Published in Bruce-Mitford, R.L.S., *Aspects of Anglo-Saxon Archaeology* (London 1974), 141–69.

Bruce-Mitford, R.L.S., *The Sutton Hoo Ship Burial* vols I-III (London 1975–83).

Campbell, J., 'The Impact of the Sutton Hoo Discovery on the Study of Anglo-Saxon History.' In Kendall, C.B. and Wells, P.S. (eds), *Voyage to the Other World*. Medieval Studies at Minnesota 5 (Minneapolis 1992), 79–101.

Carver, M., *Sutton Hoo: A seventh-century princely burial ground and its context*. Reports of the Research Committee of the Society of Antiquaries 69 (London 2005).

Evans, A.C., *The Sutton Hoo Ship Burial* (London, reprint 2002).

Heaney, S. (trans.), Donoghue, D. (ed.), *Beowulf: A verse translation* (New York, London 2002).

Masterpieces of the British Museum: The Sutton Hoo Helmet DVD (London 2007).

Meadows, I., Wollaston: 'The "Pioneer" burial.' In *Current Archaeology* 154 (1997), 391–5.

Newman, J., 'Sutton Hoo before Raedwald.' In *Current Archaeology* 180 (2002), 498–505.

Stolpe, H., *La nécropole de Vendel*. Kungl. vitterhets historie och antikvitetsakademien monographies 17 (Stockholm 1927).

Webster, L. and Meadows, I., 'Discovery of an Anglo-Saxon helmet with boar crest.' In *Minerva* 8.4 (July/August 1997), 3–5.

Williams, G., 'The circulation and function of gold coinage in conversion-period England, *c.* AD 580-680.' In Cook B.J. and Williams G. (eds) *Coinage and History in the North Sea World c. AD 500-1250: essays in honour of Marion Archibald*. The Northern World vol. 19 (Leiden, Boston 2006), 146-192.

Williams, N., 'The Sutton Hoo helmet.' In Oddy, A. (ed.), *The Art of the Conservator* (London 1992), 73–88.

Picture credits